Printed in Great Britain
by Amazon

43491026R00066